THRILLING SCIENCE AND TECHNOLOGY JOBS

ZOO VETERINARIANS

Ruth Owen and John Willis

AV2

www.av2books.com

Step 1
Go to **www.av2books.com**

Step 2
Enter this unique code
HLNJB7S1E

Step 3
Explore your interactive eBook!

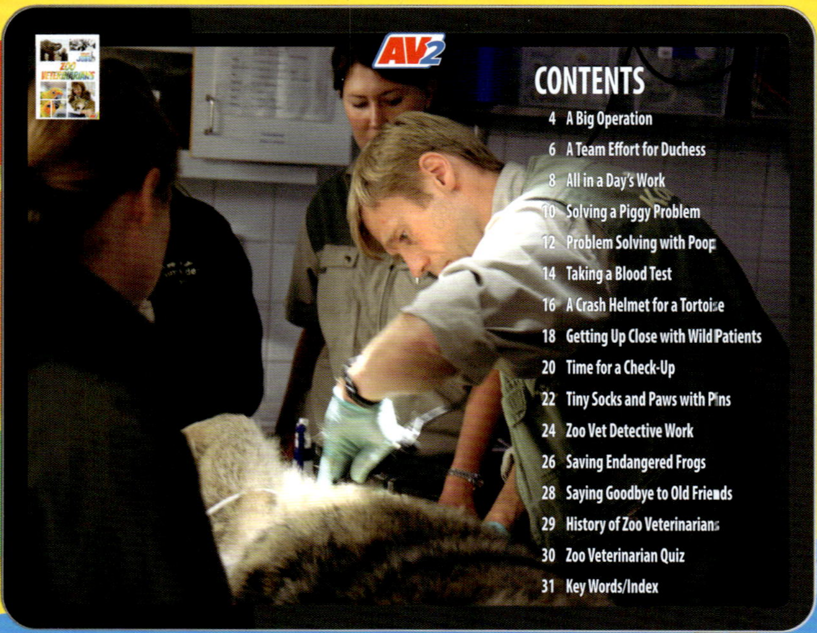

AV2 is optimized for use on any device

Your interactive eBook comes with...

Contents
Browse a live contents page to easily navigate through resources

Audio
Listen to sections of the book read aloud

Videos
Watch informative video clips

Weblinks
Gain additional information for research

Try This!
Complete activities and hands-on experiments

Key Words
Study vocabulary, and complete a matching word activity

Quizzes
Test your knowledge

Slideshows
View images and captions

... and much, much more!

THRILLING SCIENCE AND TECHNOLOGY JOBS

ZOO VETERINARIANS

Contents

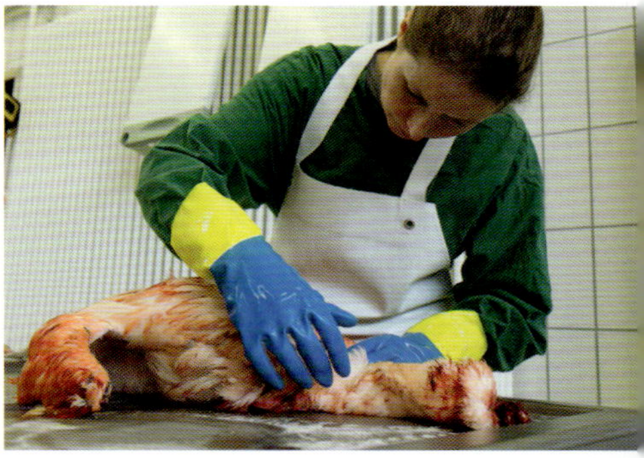

A Big Operation

It was the day of the big operation. In fact, it was to be a jumbo operation in every way! On September 20, 2012, a team of vets and nurses were preparing to carry out an eye operation.

The patient was Duchess, a 42-year-old African elephant. Duchess had already had her right eye removed. Now her left eye had **cataracts**. This condition makes the see-through lens in an eye turn cloudy. Poor Duchess could no longer see from her remaining eye.

As Duchess's keepers quietly talked to her to reassure her, zoo vet Ghislaine Sayers injected the huge elephant with a powerful dose of **general anesthetic**. Slowly, Duchess sank to her knees and then rolled onto her side. When the medical team was sure she was asleep, they quickly went to work. The operation took place in Duchess's enclosure at Paignton Zoo, in Devon, England.

During surgery on elephants, vets often give them oxygen and anesthetic gases through their mouths and trunks.

About **70 percent** of a **zoo vet's day** is spent with **animals**.

At **large zoos** such as the Smithsonian National Zoo, vets can look after more than **2,000 animals**.

Animals need **different levels** of **anesthesia** based on their **size**. **Larger animals** need **more** anesthetic.

A Team Effort for Duchess

As Duchess the elephant slept, veterinary **ophthalmologist** Jim Carter began the operation. An ophthalmologist is a vet or doctor who is an expert at treating eye diseases and problems.

To treat Duchess's cataracts, Jim used an ultrasonic handpiece. This tool makes tiny vibrations. The vibrations broke up the cataracts, or cloudy parts of the eye's lens. Then, Jim used another tool to suck the damaged tissue from the eye.

After nearly three hours, the operation was complete. Duchess was given another injection. This one contained a chemical to wake her up.

As the elephant wobbled to her feet, everyone breathed a sigh of relief. Thanks to the skills of the veterinary team, not only had Duchess survived the operation, but now she would be able to see again!

Duchess lived for seven more years after her surgery.

ZOOLOGICAL

During the operation, vets and nurses monitored Duchess's heartbeat and breathing. Each time she breathed out, they measured the amount of carbon dioxide gas in her breath. This told the team if Duchess was breathing normally or needed help.

All in a Day's Work

Just like the vets who treat our pet cats and dogs, zoo vets spend their days caring for animals. The biggest might be an elephant. The smallest could be an endangered rainforest frog or spider.

Zoo vets usually work as part of a team with other vets and veterinary nurses. The team works in the zoo's examination room and out in the animals' enclosures.

Zoo vets deal with emergencies and perform operations. They also carry out many day-to-day tasks. These include trimming hooves, **microchipping** animals, and giving the animals **vaccinations** to protect them from diseases.

Many zoo animals have a microchip under their skin. The chip contains the animal's identification number. A zoo vet uses a large needle to inject the microchip into an animal. The chip can then be read with a microchip reader.

Vaccinations are important so that animals do not spread diseases to other animals in a zoo.

Well-Known Zoos in the United States

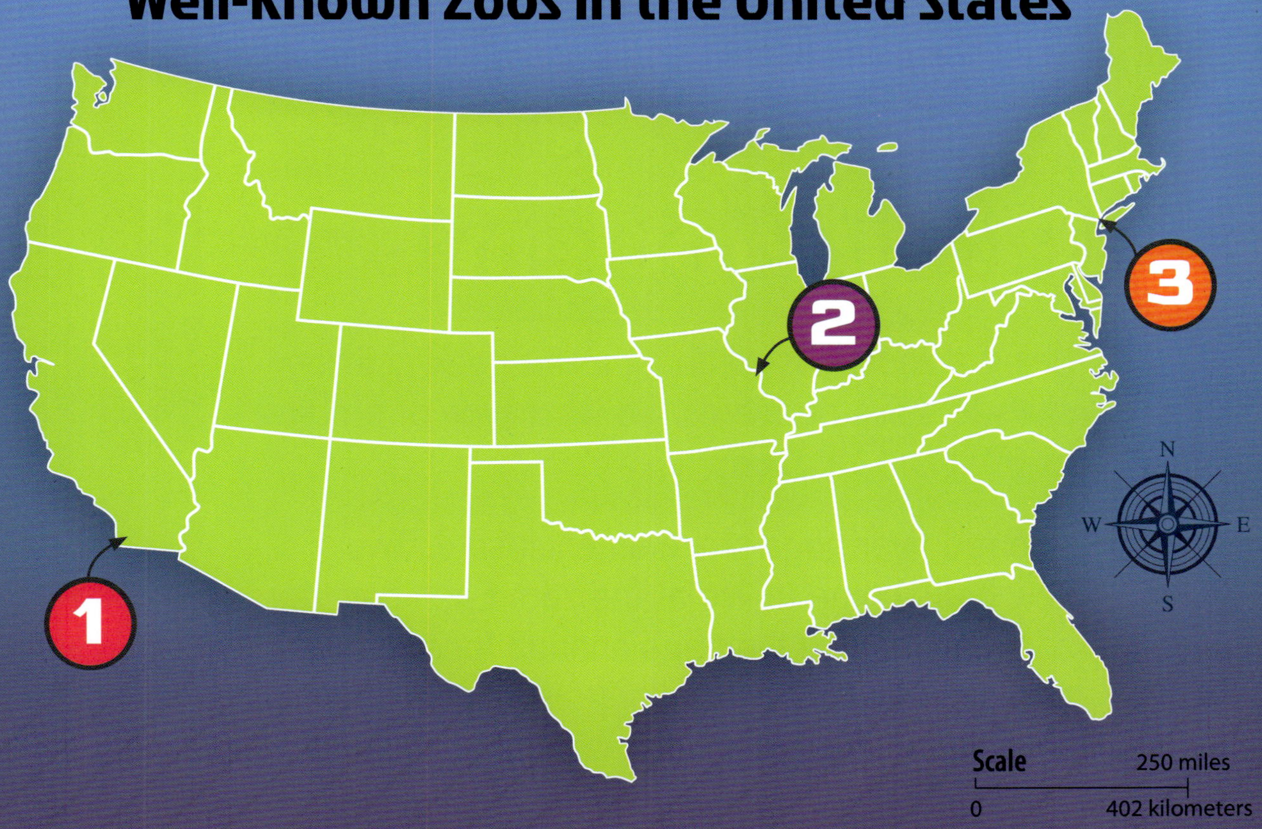

San Diego Zoo, San Diego, California
The San Diego Zoo is home to more than 3,700 animals from 650 **species**. The zoo is highly involved in conservation. In November 2019, the 100th southern white rhino from the zoo was born.

Saint Louis Zoo, St. Louis, Missouri
The Saint Louis Zoo celebrates its 110th year in 2020. One of the zoo's main attractions is a train that stops at popular animal exhibits. The Saint Louis zoo is environmentally conscious and bans plastic bags.

Bronx Zoo, New York City, New York
The Bronx Zoo is one of the largest in the United States, at 265 acres. It sees more than 2.15 million visitors each year. The Bronx Zoo is home to 4,000 animals from 650 species.

Solving a Piggy Problem

Being a zoo vet is all about using good science skills to solve problems. So what type of problem might a zoo vet face?

Two red river hogs share an enclosure. Two new hogs come to live at the zoo. Each day, the zookeepers give the hogs enough food for four animals. The two original hogs start to look thin, however. Why are the hogs losing weight?

The vet observes the animals to see if they seem ill or in pain. The vet weighs the hogs and checks them against a chart that gives scores for certain body conditions. The vet's research shows that the two hogs are thin but not unwell. The vet wonders whether the new hogs might be bullying the thin hogs and stealing their food.

The zoo vet asks the hogs' keepers to feed the two thin hogs away from their greedy housemates. Once a week, the vet weighs the thin hogs. After four weeks, the weight data shows that the thin hogs are now gaining weight.

The two new hogs were stealing the thin hogs' food. Problem solved.

Red river hogs typically weigh about 100 to 285 pounds (45 to 129 kilograms).

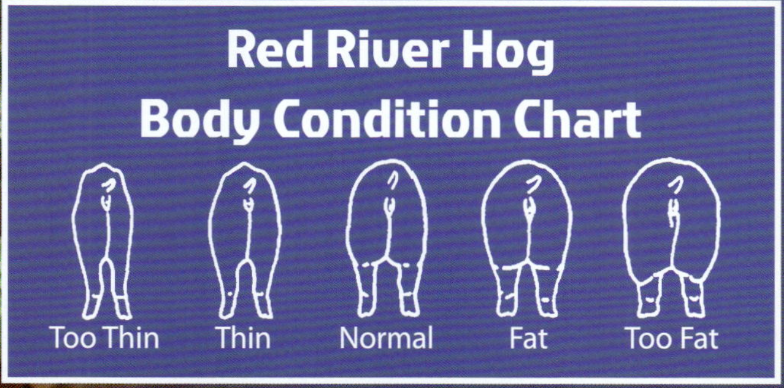

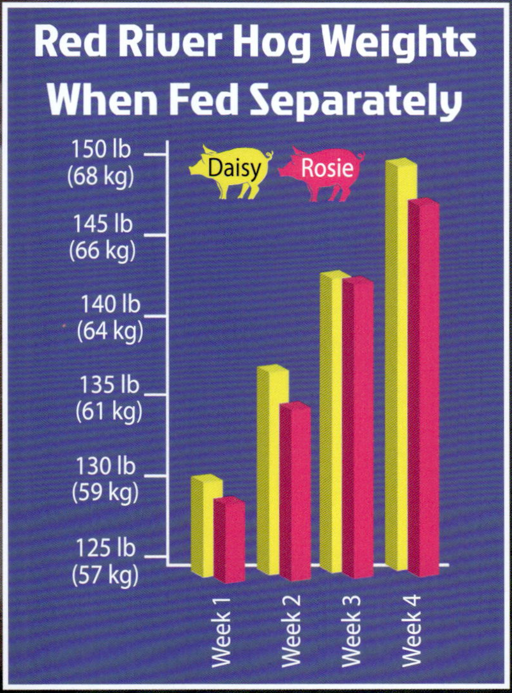

ZOOLOGICAL

Zoo animals are trained by their keepers to climb onto scales to be weighed. Once an animal is on the scales, it is rewarded with a food treat.

Problem Solving with Poop

It may sound gross, but examining dung, or poop, is all part of a zoo vet's job.

Many animals have **parasites**, such as roundworms, in their stomachs. The worms lay their eggs in an animal's stomach. Then, the eggs are passed out when the animal poops. If an animal has too many worms, it can become sick.

To test for parasitic worms, a keeper collects samples of dung. Then, the zoo vet examines the dung under a **microscope**.

The vet looks for **microscopic** worm eggs and **larvae**. If there are lots of eggs and larvae, it means the animal has too many worms.

The zoo vet might give the animal a worming injection to kill off the parasites, or some medicine mixed into its food.

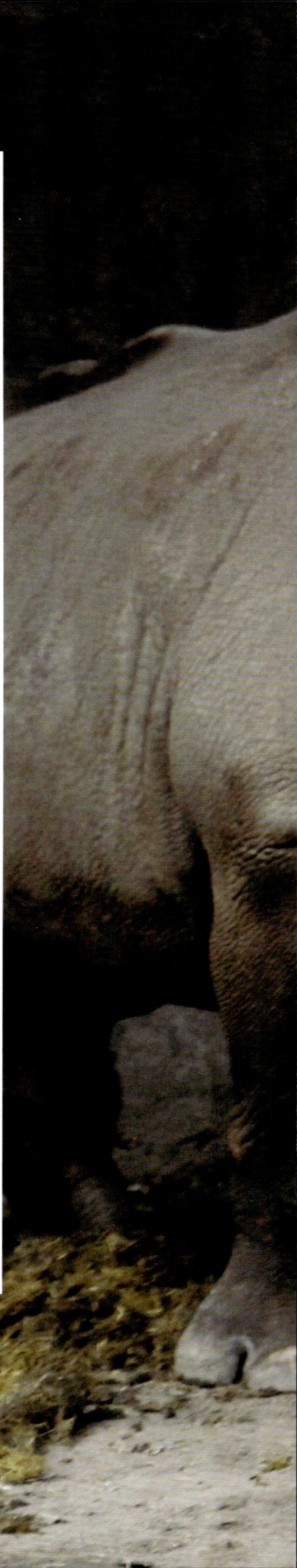

Keepers collect dung from an animal for three days to have the best chance of finding parasites in the samples.

Microscopes can magnify samples up to 1,000 times.

ZOOLOGICAL

In some enclosures it can be tricky to know whose poop is whose. If just one animal needs a dung test, that animal is fed food mixed with edible glitter—the kind that is used for decorating cupcakes. Once some sparkly poop appears, the keeper knows that is the stuff for testing!

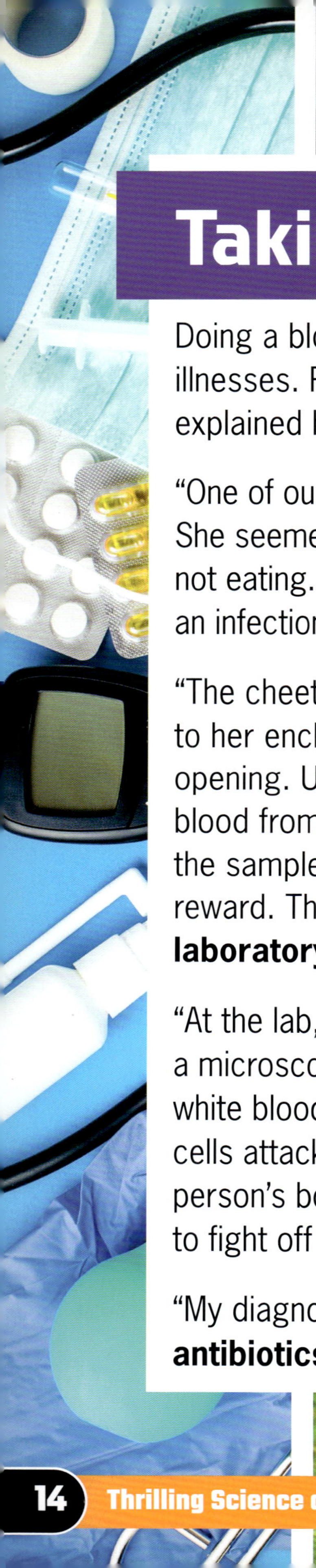

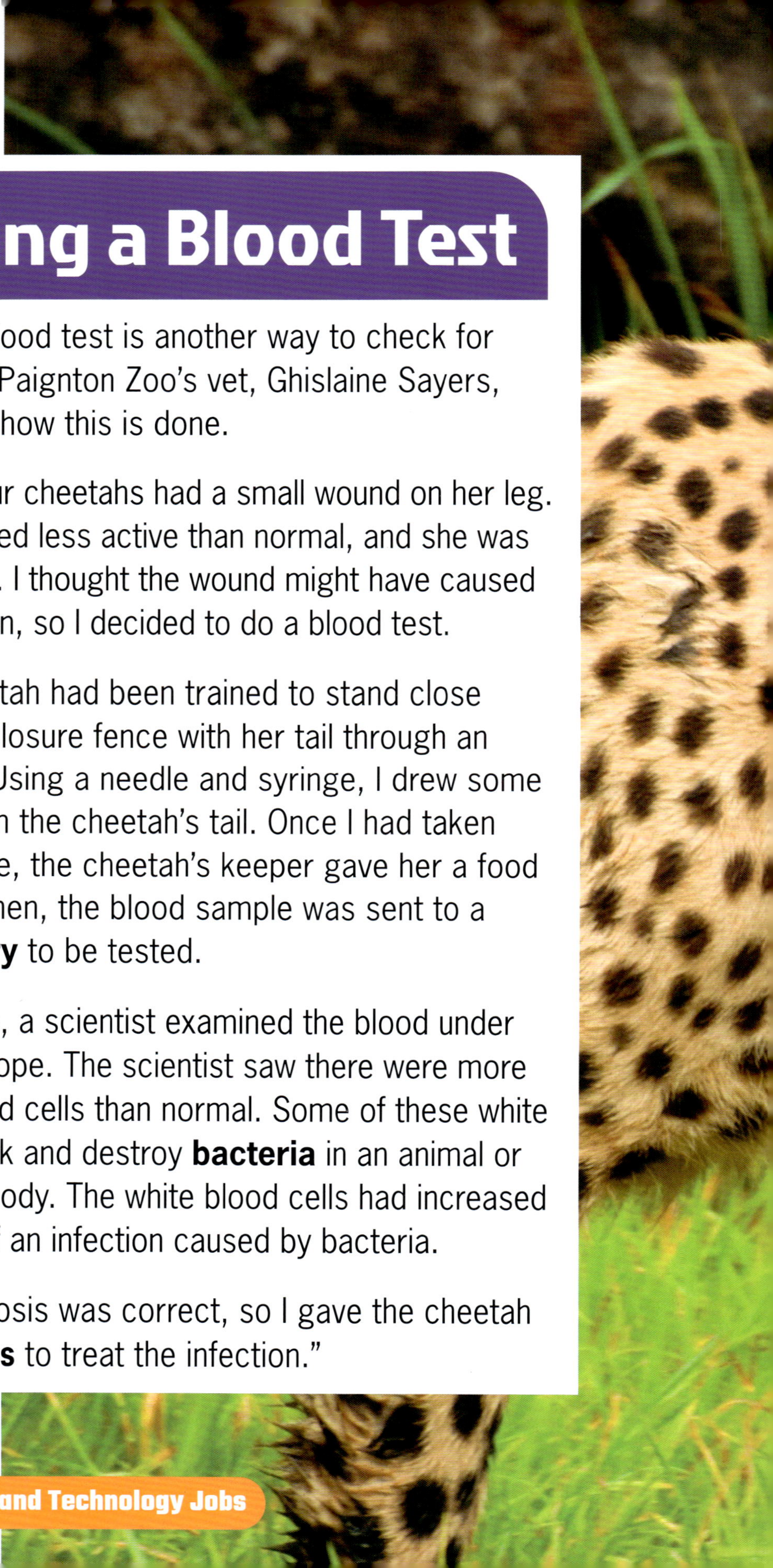

Taking a Blood Test

Doing a blood test is another way to check for illnesses. Paignton Zoo's vet, Ghislaine Sayers, explained how this is done.

"One of our cheetahs had a small wound on her leg. She seemed less active than normal, and she was not eating. I thought the wound might have caused an infection, so I decided to do a blood test.

"The cheetah had been trained to stand close to her enclosure fence with her tail through an opening. Using a needle and syringe, I drew some blood from the cheetah's tail. Once I had taken the sample, the cheetah's keeper gave her a food reward. Then, the blood sample was sent to a **laboratory** to be tested.

"At the lab, a scientist examined the blood under a microscope. The scientist saw there were more white blood cells than normal. Some of these white cells attack and destroy **bacteria** in an animal or person's body. The white blood cells had increased to fight off an infection caused by bacteria.

"My diagnosis was correct, so I gave the cheetah **antibiotics** to treat the infection."

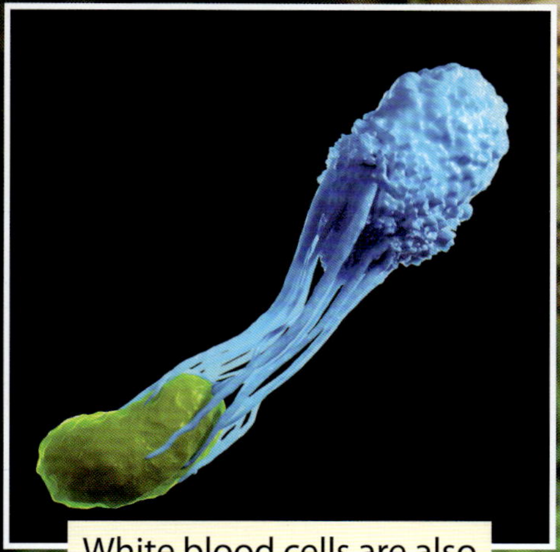

White blood cells are also known as leucocytes.

Cheetahs are the fastest land animal in the world. They can run up to 75 miles (121 kilometers) per hour.

ZOOLOGICAL

Many zoo animals are trained by their keepers to have medical treatments. The animals learn to touch an object, such as a red plastic ball, and then remain still. When the treatment is over, the animal receives a food reward.

A Crash Helmet for a Tortoise

Some problems faced by zoo vets can be solved with just a little creative thinking.

One day, a giant tortoise at Paignton Zoo suffered a bad wound and ended up with a large hole in his shell. Zoo vet Ghislaine Sayers cleaned the wound with an **antiseptic** liquid to remove any dirt and kill any bacteria. Then, Sayers applied **dressings** to the wound.

It is not possible, however, to stitch up a hole in a shell. So a member of the zoo's maintenance team made a section of fake shell from fiberglass. Then, Sayers used duct tape to hold the fake shell in place.

The tortoise's shell would grow back in about 18 months. Until then, he would wear his new crash helmet!

A tortoise shell has three parts. The top is called the carapace, and the bottom is the plastron. The bridge connects the other two parts.

Just like doctors for humans, zoo vets use supplies including antiseptics, stitches, and bandages to heal animals.

ZOOLOGICAL

Zoo vets sometimes have to treat animals that are wounded in fights. Animals fight over food, nesting areas, or the best sunbathing spots. Male animals also fight over females.

Getting Up Close with Wild Patients

Zoo vets often have to get close to potentially dangerous animals.

To safely do this, a vet may anesthetize an animal with a dart gun. From outside the animal's enclosure, the vet shoots a dart into the animal. When the needle part of the dart pierces the animal's skin, anesthetic pumps from the needle. Within a few minutes, the animal is asleep.

Zoo vets practice shooting dart guns. They must be good shots as animals quickly become scared or panicked. Also, a vet must dart an animal in an area where there is lots of muscle, such as its shoulder or bottom. The vet must avoid hitting nerves, blood vessels, the animal's eyes, or small, delicate bones.

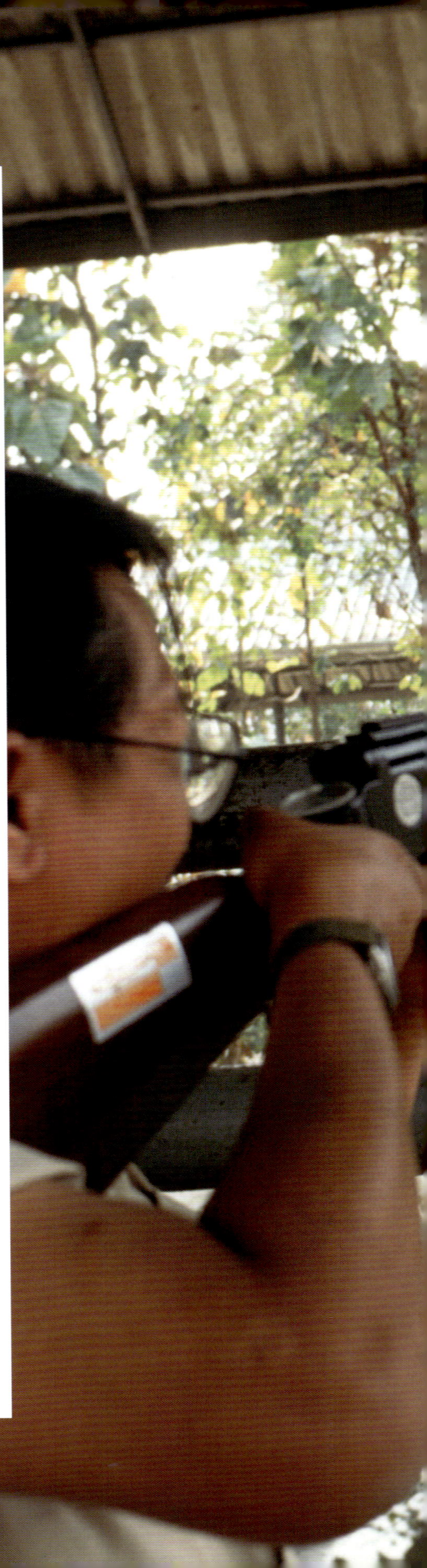

Because animals have different sizes and structures, each one needs a different dose of tranquilizer.

Dart guns are pressurized with CO_2 so that the dart will hit its target.

ZOOLOGICAL

No animal likes to be hit with a dart. A chimpanzee, however, may become very angry and throw the dart back at the vet! So, after darting a chimp, the vet quickly moves away from the enclosure.

Time for a Check-Up

One of the reasons an animal may be anesthetized is for a check-up. Older animals especially need regular health checks.

The vet begins by asking an animal's keeper lots of questions about its behavior and day-to-day life. For example, is it eating normally? Does it sometimes have wet fur around its mouth? This could mean the animal is dribbling because its teeth are causing pain.

Next, every part of the animal is examined, including its eyes, mouth, nose, skin, hair, or feathers.

The vet listens to the animal's heart with a **stethoscope** to make sure the animal's heartbeat is normal. The vet also listens for how the air is flowing through the animal's lungs.

An x-ray machine may be used to check the animal's bones and joints.

The word *stethoscope* means "I see the chest."

X-rays can also be used to figure out the age of an animal.

ZOOLOGICAL

In the wild, a sick animal may become a target for predators. So wild animals are very good at hiding illness and injuries. This makes it difficult for zoo vets to spot when an animal is unwell.

Tiny Socks and Paws with Pins

A peek into a zoo's veterinary center can sometimes reveal a few surprises. You might see a lion that looks like a pin cushion or a monkey wearing odd stripy socks!

Lucifer the lion's foot was very painful after having a growth removed. Zoo vet Nicki Grint used a treatment called **acupuncture** on the huge cat. Nicki stuck dozens of pins into Lucifer's paw. When correctly positioned, the pins help soothe pain.

When an animal is under anesthetic, its body gets cold. It loses heat through its hands and feet. Ghislaine Sayers and her team came up with a cute but practical solution. The animal's feet or hands are wrapped in bubble wrap and then covered with socks.

Zoo staff members often find socks lost by babies or small children on the zoo grounds. These tiny socks are just right for keeping a monkey's hands and feet warm.

Monkeys have human-like hands. This is why their fingers can get cold easily.

There are only **four people** on Earth who know how to do acupuncture on penguins.

Acupuncture and **herbal remedies** are becoming **more popular** at zoos. The **Singapore Zoo** has treated **200 animals** with these methods.

A database called **Zoological Information Management System (ZIMS)** keeps records on **thousands of animals** and their **reactions** to medical treatments.

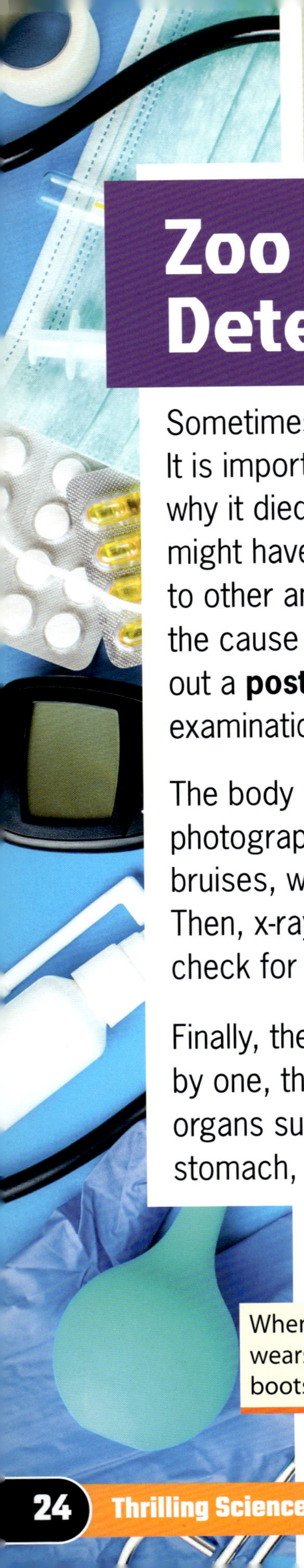

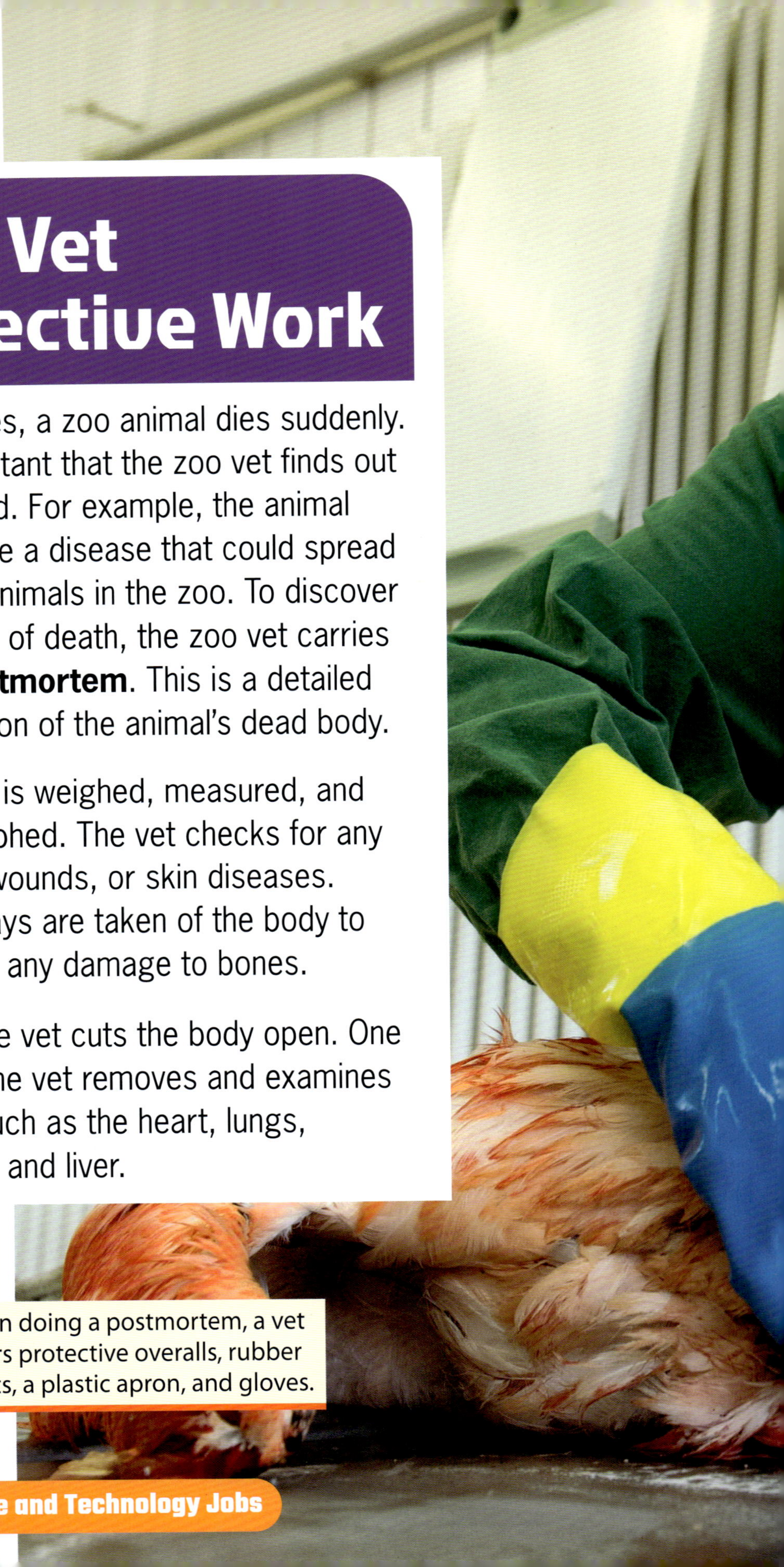

Zoo Vet Detective Work

Sometimes, a zoo animal dies suddenly. It is important that the zoo vet finds out why it died. For example, the animal might have a disease that could spread to other animals in the zoo. To discover the cause of death, the zoo vet carries out a **postmortem**. This is a detailed examination of the animal's dead body.

The body is weighed, measured, and photographed. The vet checks for any bruises, wounds, or skin diseases. Then, x-rays are taken of the body to check for any damage to bones.

Finally, the vet cuts the body open. One by one, the vet removes and examines organs such as the heart, lungs, stomach, and liver.

When doing a postmortem, a vet wears protective overalls, rubber boots, a plastic apron, and gloves.

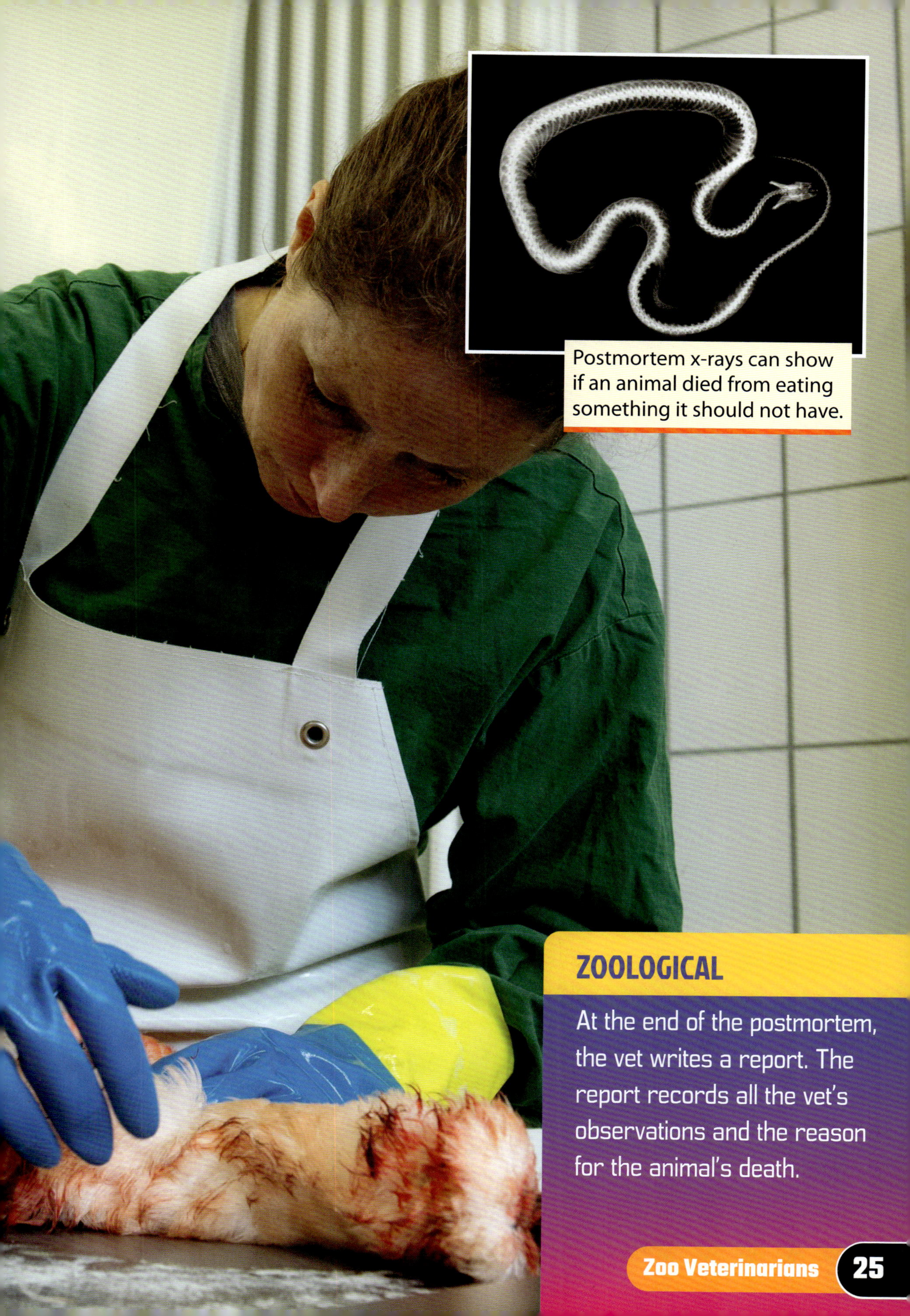

Postmortem x-rays can show if an animal died from eating something it should not have.

ZOOLOGICAL

At the end of the postmortem, the vet writes a report. The report records all the vet's observations and the reason for the animal's death.

Saving Endangered Frogs

A very important part of a zoo vet's job is to help protect endangered animals.

Around the world, hundreds of species of frogs are in danger of extinction. People have cut down the rainforests where many frogs live. They have also allowed chemicals and other pollution to contaminate rivers and ponds.

Every frog species around the world is threatened by a fast-spreading, deadly disease. The disease is caused by a type of fungus called chytrid.

The zookeepers and veterinary team at Paignton Zoo are helping to save frogs. They breed frogs, such as the critically endangered golden mantella frog.

Members of the Paignton Zoo team study frog diseases. They also study frog habitats and how frogs live. This research is passed onto **conservationists** who help protect frogs in the wild.

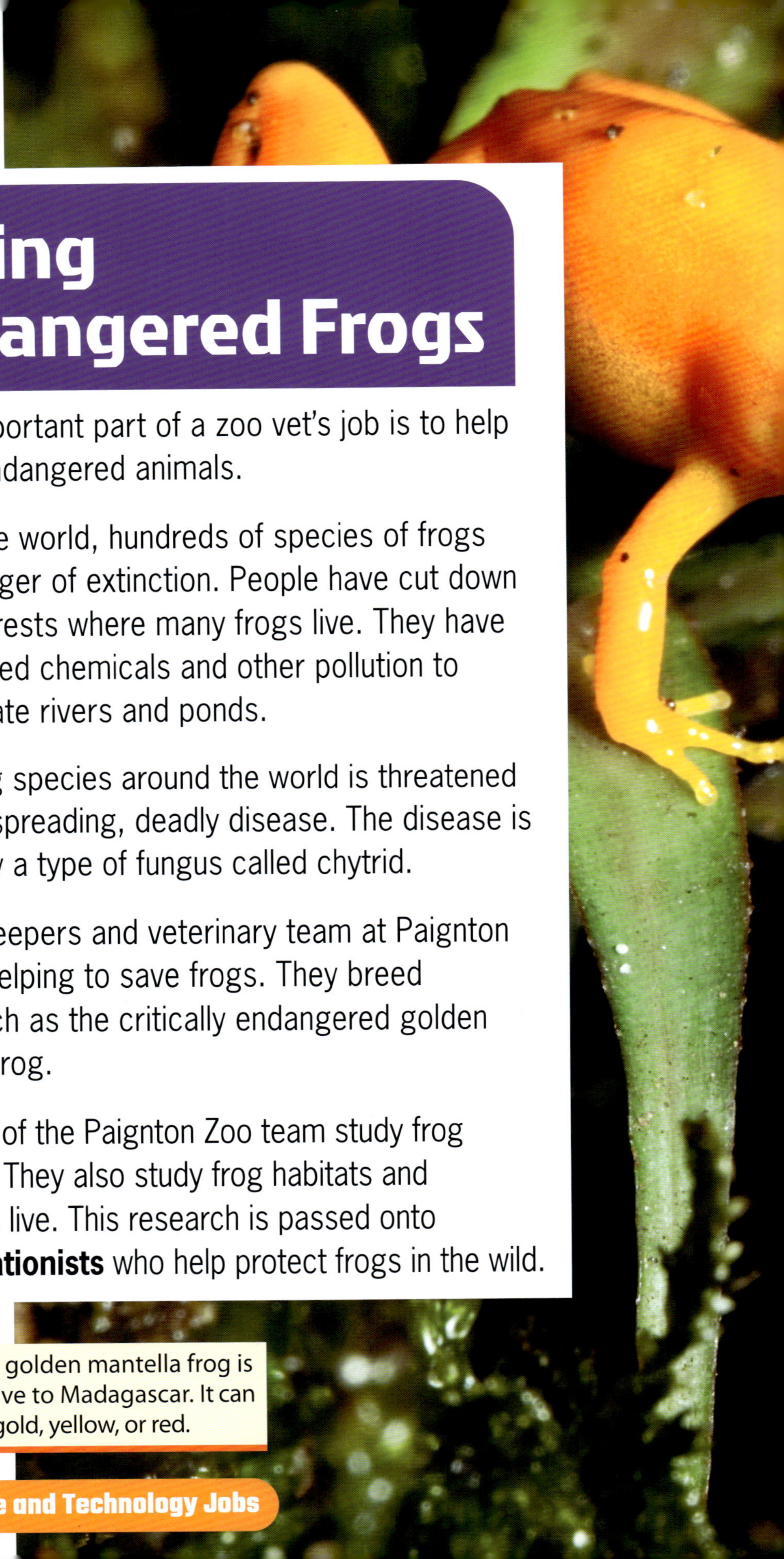

The golden mantella frog is native to Madagascar. It can be gold, yellow, or red.

Golden mantellas are often caught as pets. This is one reason why they are threatened with extinction.

ZOOLOGICAL

Paignton Zoo's frogs are kept in a bio-secure unit. This means they are protected from diseases and the outside world. Before working with the frogs, the keepers and vets must change into clean, contamination-free overalls.

Saying Goodbye to Old Friends

Around the world, zoos are breeding endangered animals. Zoos work together to match up animals with partners for breeding. Once a good match is made, one member of the animal pair must move from its old home to be with its new mate.

A zoo vet must be sure an animal does not have a disease that could spread to animals in its new home. The animal must also be healthy enough to make a long, stressful journey. The vet tests the animal's dung and blood to make sure it has no diseases. When a new animal arrives at a zoo, the vet carries out the same checks.

At a large zoo, there may be animals leaving and new ones arriving every month. Saying goodbye to old animal friends, and welcoming new ones, is all part of a zoo vet's work.

Sometimes, animals are shipped from war-torn countries and rehoused at zoos.

History of Zoo Veterinarians

The history of zoo vets began with the creation of zoos and veterinary medicine. Today, zoo vets are the backbone of the zoo and care deeply about the animals they are surrounded by.

1500 BC Queen Hatshepsut of Egypt creates the first public zoo by collecting animals from across Africa.

1828–1847 AD The first modern zoos for educational purposes open in London, England, Paris, France, Dublin, Ireland, and Halifax, Nova Scotia.

1946 The American Association of Zoo Veterinarians (AAZV) is founded.

1957 David Taylor becomes the first veterinarian to specialize in zoo and wildlife medicine and surgery.

1974 The ZIMS database is created.

March 2000 *The Journal of Zoo and Wildlife Medicine* releases its first issue. Still publishing today, the journal prints articles about zoology and veterinary medicine.

2013 Bob Barker, a former TV game show host and animal rights activist, pays to move three African elephants from the Toronto Zoo to Performing Animal Welfare Society's (PAWS) sanctuary in California.

2019 Joanne Paul-Murphy wins the 2019 American Veterinary Medical Association (AVMA) Animal Welfare Award for her work advancing the medical treatment of birds.

Zoo Veterinarian Quiz

01 Who was the first person to become a zoo vet?

02 What does a zoo vet have to do before an animal goes to another zoo?

03 What does a zoo vet do when an animal dies?

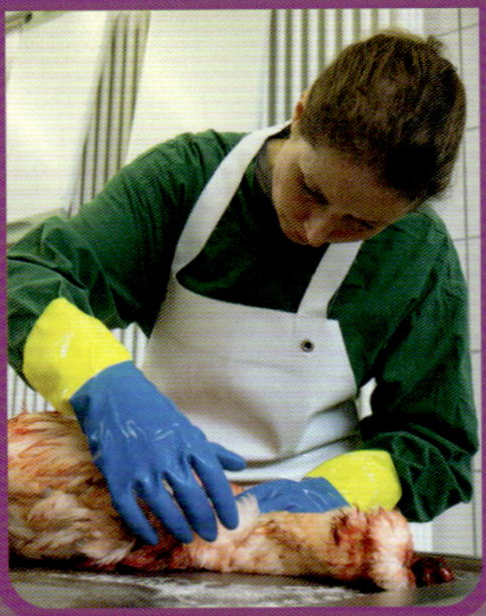

04 Why do monkeys need socks during surgeries?

05 What do zoo vets do to check for illnesses?

06 What is the system that was created as a database for zoo vets to see animal's reactions to various treatments?

07 Which California zoo is home to about 3,700 animals?

08 What percentage of a zoo vet's day is spent with animals?

09 What does a zoo vet use to hear an animal's heart and lungs?

10 What is a conservationist?

ANSWER

01 David Taylor **02** Make sure it is healthy enough to travel and has no diseases **03** Postmortem **04** They get cold hands and feet **05** Look at blood and dung samples **06** Zoological Information Management System (ZIMS) **07** San Diego Zoo **08** 70 percent **09** Stethoscope **10** Someone who works to protect animals and the environment

Key Words

acupuncture: an ancient medical treatment from China in which long, thin needles are inserted into the skin at particular points

antibiotics: medicines, such as injections or pills, that kill or stop the growth of the bacteria that cause infections

antiseptic: able to kill off bacteria

bacteria: microscopic living things. Some bacteria are helpful, while others can cause disease.

cataracts: cloudy areas in the lens of an eye that make it difficult to see

conservationists: persons who do work to protect wild animals, plants, and natural habitats

dressings: materials such as bandages that are used to cover a wound

general anesthetic: a chemical that is injected into or is breathed in by a person or animal. It makes patients become unconscious and stops them from feeling pain.

laboratory: a room or building where there is equipment that can be used to carry out experiments and other scientific studies

larvae: the young of some animals. A larva usually looks like a worm.

microchipping: injecting a tiny device, the size of a grain of rice, into an animal. The microchip contains information about the animal that can be read by a microchip reader.

microscopes: a tool or machine that is used to see things that are too small to see with the eyes alone

microscopic: only visible when viewed through a microscope

ophthalmologist: a doctor or vet who specializes in treating eye problems

parasites: living things that live on and get their food from other living things

postmortem: an in-depth examination of a dead body to find out why an animal or person died

species: different types of living things. The members of an animal species look alike and can produce young together.

stethoscope: a medical instrument used for listening to sounds from inside an animal or person's body

vaccinations: substances that are injected into animals or persons to give protection against diseases

Index

Get the best of both worlds.

AV2 bridges the gap between print and digital.

The expandable resources toolbar enables quick access to content including **videos**, **audio**, **activities**, **weblinks**, **slideshows**, **quizzes**, and **key words**.

Animated videos make static images come alive.

Resource icons on each page help readers to further **explore key concepts**.

Published by AV2
350 5th Avenue, 59th Floor
New York, NY 10118
Website: www.av2books.com

Library of Congress Control Number: 2019957554

ISBN 978-1-7911-2187-7 (hardcover)
ISBN 978-1-7911-2188-4 (softcover)
ISBN 978-1-7911-2189-1 (multi-user eBook)
ISBN 978-1-7911-2190-7 (single-user eBook)

Printed in Guangzhou, China
1 2 3 4 5 6 7 8 9 0 24 23 22 21 20

032020
101319

Project Coordinator: John Willis
Designer: Terry Paulhus

AV2 acknowledges Alamy, Getty Images, iStock, Minden Pictures, Newscom, and Shutterstock as its primary image suppliers for this title.

First published in 2016 by Ruby Tuesday Books Ltd.